D1270368

21st Century
Basic Skills
Library

I KNOW
BASKETBALL

by Annabelle Tometich

Cherry Lake Publishing • Ann Arbor, Michigan

3

Published in the United States of America
by Cherry Lake Publishing
Ann Arbor, Michigan
www.cherrylakepublishing.com

Consultant: Marla Conn, Read-Ability

Photo Credits: Lane V. Erickson/Shutterstock, cover, 1 ; iStockphoto/
Thinkstock, 4; Quang Ho/Shutterstock, 6; AP Images, 8; Aspen Photo/
Shutterstock, 10; Konstantin L/Shutterstock, 12; Lorraine Swanson/
Shutterstock, 14; AP Images, 16; Mark J. Terrill/AP Images, 18; Reed
Saxon/AP Images, 20

Library of Congress Cataloging-in-Publication Data
Tometich, Annabelle, 1980-
  I know basketball / Annabelle Tometich.
     pages cm. -- (I know sports)
  Includes index.
  ISBN 978-1-62431-398-1 (hardcover) -- ISBN 978-1-62431-474-2 (pbk.) --
ISBN 978-1-62431-436-0 (pdf) -- ISBN 978-1-62431-512-1 (ebook)
  1. Basketball--Juvenile literature. I. Title.
  GV885.1.T66 2013
  796.323--dc23
                                        2013006122

Cherry Lake Publishing would like to acknowledge
the work of The Partnership for 21st Century Skills.
Please visit *www.p21.org* for more information.

Printed in the United States of America
Corporate Graphics Inc.
July 2013
CLFA11

TABLE OF CONTENTS

History

Basketball became a sport in 1891. A gym teacher invented it. His students could then play a sport inside.

Players scored points by throwing a ball into a peach basket. The game had only 13 rules.

The National Basketball Association (NBA) began in 1949. It had 17 teams. Today it has 30.

Rules

Two teams play against each other on a **court**. Five players from each team play at a time.

A **hoop** is at each end of the court. Players score points by **shooting** the basketball through the hoop. The team with the most points at the end of the game wins.

Basketball players **dribble** the ball. They can shoot it. They can also pass it. They cannot run with the ball.

Records

Wilt Chamberlain scored 100 points in a game in 1962. No player in the NBA has broken this record.

Kobe Bryant came close. He scored 81 points in a game in 2006.

Kareem Abdul-Jabbar scored 38,387 points during his **career**. It is still an NBA record.

Find Out More

BOOK

Woods, Mark. *Basketball Legends*. New York: Crabtree, 2009.

WEB SITE

Sports Illustrated Kids

www.sikids.com

This Web site has articles about professional basketball and NBA players.

Glossary

career (kuh-REER) the work a person has

court (KORT) the place where basketball is played

dribble (DRIB-uhl) to bounce a basketball while walking or running

hoop (HOOP) a metal ring with an open net attached to the bottom

shooting (SHOO-ting) tossing a basketball toward the hoop

Home and School Connection

Use this list of words from the book to help your child become a better reader. Word games and writing activities can help beginning readers reinforce literacy skills.

against	game	pass	students
ball	gym	peach	teacher
basket	has	players	team
basketball	hoop	points	then
became	inside	record	throwing
began	into	rules	time
broken	invented	run	today
career	it	scored	wins
dribble	only	shoot	
each	other	sport	

Index

About the Author

Annabelle Tometich worked as a sportswriter at the *News-Press* in Fort Myers, Florida, for six years, winning five awards from the Associated Press Sports Editors. She has also written for the U.S. Olympic Committee's Web site, TeamUSA.org. She lives in Fort Myers with her husband and son.